In the golden days of Greek civilization, four hundred years ... opher Plato wrote the *Di*... the most influential body ... l. Written in the form of ... h philosophy's continual ... na of intellectual conflict. ... on of the ideal state, presents Plato's ... ation, justice, and the philosopher-king, the wise and just prototype of a ruler who could cure the world's ills. In the dialogues *Apology*, *Crito*, and *Phaedo*, the imposing figure of Socrates, Plato's beloved mentor, emerges to discuss respect for law and authority, human virtue, and the immortality of the soul. The additional dialogues contain the great philosopher's thinking on subjects of such universal and ageless interest as art, virtue, and the nature of love and beauty.

W. H. D. Rouse, one of the world's greatest classical scholars, made world-famous translations of Homer's *The Odyssey* and *The Iliad*. Dr. Rouse was educated at Cambridge University, where he became an Honorary Fellow of Christ's College.

Matthew S. Santirocco is Professor of Classics and Dean of the College of Arts and Science at New York University. He has written on Greek and Roman literature and edits the journal *Classical World*.

Rebecca Newberger Goldstein is the author of such novels as *The Mind-Body Problem*; *Properties of Light: A Novel of Love, Betrayal, and Quantum Physics*; and *36 Arguments for the Existence of God: A Work of Fiction*; as well as acclaimed nonfiction including *Betraying Spinoza: The Renegade Jew Who Gave Us Modernity* and *Plato at the Googleplex: Why Philosophy Won't Go Away*. Among her many honors and awards are a Guggenheim Fellowship, a MacArthur Fellowship, and grants from the National Science Foundation and the American Council of Learned Societies. She was named Humanist of the Year by the American Humanist Association and elected to the American Academy of Arts and Sciences. She is currently Visiting Professor of Philosophy, New College of the Humanities, London.